HOW TO PRAY IN PITTSBURGH

Charlotte Lit Press
Charlotte Center for Literary Arts, Inc.
PO Box 18607
Charlotte, NC 28218
charlottelit.org/press

Cover photo by Vivian I. Bikulege
Author photo by Dana Bernard

ISBN: 978-1-960558-08-4

HOW TO PRAY IN PITTSBURGH

Vivian I. Bikulege

CHARLOTTELIT PRESS

Charlotte Center for Literary Arts, Inc.
Charlotte, North Carolina
charlottelit.org

To

my husband Mac, my heart,
my mother Irene, my soul,
my dad Stan, my guiding light,
Stacie and Stanley, beloved sibling sojourners,
and
family, friends, and companion poets.

I love you.

Contents

Find Me

Find me in predawn quiet, groggy in prayer,
a lit candle, coffee.

Find me in front of my bathroom mirror,
my hair foreign, my teeth dull.

Find me in a pool wishing I could do a flip turn.

Find me in the grocery store judging bananas,
wanton for chips, tempted by Havarti cheese.

Find me in a hurry, calling a friend,
trying to make time for some time.

Find me in church wanting to love everyone,
knowing it is impossible.

Find me in my desk chair typing gibberish,
wondering if anyone will call this poetry.

Find me in a dream where my husband is the hero,
and my family saves the day.

Find me in sadness knowing I must pull myself up.
To where? For whom? Why?

Find me in contemplation at day's end,
excavating crumbled gratitude.

Find me in a sleeping bag, cocooning nylon and down,
zipped in my own warm breath.

A Beckoning

Terrier tugs
& the beagle's bugle leads
walk after walk,
I consider death. Mine.

On our path that fallen tree.
It rots, rib cage splinters soft,
shapeless, becomes pulp,
home to a blight of fungus.

My hair whispers white, curious
skin crepes—a beckoning
to lie down on the earth. Decay.

Beagle returns,
terrier heels,
their eyes fixed on my fist
full of crunchy treats.

We turn our backs on marsh woods,
pant, breathe, crave water.
A great blue heron lifts,
day lights promise.

Lea's Wedding Gown

Generations sewn together: her mother's chiffon swept
into the free flow of a skirt, as aging satin
from her godmother's gown drips a sequined trail
on a train southbound to a Georgian altar.

Tulle resurrects
from her grandmother's bargain basement bridal dress
into a veil of gauze petals,
blooms breezy atop her blonde curls,
lifts in a silent swirl like smoke wisps from a genie's lamp.

Inside Faith Chapel, invisible threads even out her hem.
French lace, intricate as a spider's weave
adorns her hands and arms,
compels the groom to whisper, *I like your sleeves.*

Silk buttons, an invisible zipper, secure skin's sparks of joy.
Promises tied in a white bustle's bow tether tomorrow.
Will the years ahead be as beautiful?

Caught in a Tangle

September night:
my move from low country palms
to poplar and river birch—
a fresh cut.

First mountain sighting—a spider
frames the door corner in web.
He is centered.
I am not.

My porch light illumines
his silky weave,
a crane fly exhausts
in the tangle.

A rescue mission? No.
To meddle in nature's course
seems useless. I muffle my heart,
Hush.

Night two: The web sways sliced.
No spider in retreat, no prey
struggles to survive a spiral.
I turn off the light.

Night three: Flick the switch.
Blue Ridge Spiderman arcs
through crisp air,
mends his mottled web

stronger, whole
until gossamer dew and dawn
bedeck the delicate net
in water pearls of first light.

Brown Soldiers

Age is a battle, and I am a prisoner of war.

Eyebrow troops have deserted my face.
Only a squad remains,
meager survivors of two platoons,
thin brown soldiers left to stand at attention
along the eroding cliff of my forehead.

I pencil in reserves—Maybelline Company.
The rims of my eyeglasses will camouflage
those missing in action.

Everyday Swim

Early morning: I pull my body through water,
right arm stronger than left.

Together they tow because my feet will forget
to flutter kick.

I cut a wake through still water,
ripple in a new day,

tilt my head right, inhale,
turn my face down

to the deep
until the glide ends.

Asymptomatic

Invisible,
hidden like hushed sin
carried like dried sweat under arms
but odorless, a ghost's scent, unseen, unspoken
a mute infection spreads—lovers' touch, breath, a kiss,
fingerprints left on shopping carts, a fuel nozzle, loose change.
It isn't always disease; forgotten kindness mutates, sharp words
grow teeth, go viral, socialize, digitize. An entire planet sickens,
isolates, hoards, denies. Hate doesn't rest on microscope slides.
Vaccines only work for a while. Test, retest, positive, negative
broadcast, accuse, confuse. Return to ancient alphabets
to name a phantom, a plague—loneliness. We fester.
No feet apart, six feet apart, meters, miles …
mask, double mask, N-95
intubate, ventilate
hide.

Legacy

Hand-rolled balls of string
in a Thom McAn shoebox,

nuts and bolts stow away
in plastic Jif jars,

and green No. 2 pencils lean
in a chipped coffee mug.

A black metal dustpan and horsehair brush
crossed state lines from Dad's workbench to mine.

On pegboard a hacksaw, screwdrivers,
a ball peen hammer for picture hooks.

Hold it straight, like this …
his hand curled 'round mine,

his voice an echo
inside secondhand smoke.

Scraps of him clutter my garage.

On Another Tuesday Night

Isn't this enough? To read books together in bed.
You read yours. I read mine.
Again: *Isn't this enough?*

Yes is no answer.

I lift the bedcovers, plant my body,
read a sentence from my book
with no comprehension of it or us.
As I age, I wrestle away any sense of peace.

Wasn't there a time when a day without sex
was a day wasted? When we thumbed our noses
in shameless acts of hot protest,
erotic tumbles and acrobatics.
We'd perform every day,
with or without a license or church blessing.

Back then, were we held hostage by Lust?
Did Love wait by the dance floor in a folding chair—
too shy to cut in, too proper to grind in raw gyrations?

Tonight, Love is mist on our bedroom landscape.
Under Egyptian cotton, atop feather pillows,
she exhales in silent meditation. Warm lips,
hands & fingers poised to light a fire.
And by this I mean, I could love you
in quiet conversation and touch.

If you turn that next page
and leave me to smolder,
my spark could burn down
every necessary thing.

Time Sounds Like Crickets

When the heat comes on, there's a rattle in the house. My husband says it sounds like crickets and depends on me to remedy the situation. The thought of tracing ductwork under a cold house fatigues me. Yesterday, we made love, but I didn't come. He didn't help me along or wait for me, just asked, *Are you okay? Do you want me to play with you?* I did, but I said no.

Today, I blew leaves from my neighbor's driveway. Charlie can hardly walk. His wife has the flu. In her blue robe and worn moccasins, she watches me work. She needs a haircut. Long hair on older women can be intentional or tired. Too tired to dye. Too sick to clear the driveway. Too *I don't give a shit* to hang a Christmas wreath on her front door. Leaves will grow back in the spring. If she cuts her hair, it will grow back too.

Back home, between the rattle and ticking clocks, I read Tony Hoagland's poetry, the last stanzas he wrote before giving in to pancreatic cancer. Could I die at 64 like he did? That means time's up. I am selfish with my time. I try to hoard it, but it's impossible.

Warm air rattles. Clocks tick. I'm in a Lazy Boy thinking about standing. There are crickets I need to put to sleep.

In Anticipation of Winter

My clitoris has disappeared,
and I do not know if I want it
to come out of hiding.

My priest doesn't care if I ever find it,
and I am unsure if my husband knows
it is missing, so rare
his attempts to play
hide and seek.

So, I'll croon
between Cold and Wolf full moons.
          Ollie, ollie in-come-free …
and wait, anticipate
a delicious kiss,
          his naked body pressed to mine,
                    a gentle fingertip.

Dog Down

At Milepost 331
on the Blue Ridge Parkway,
a curious couple wanders
toward our Winnebago.

Nice rig, the man calls out.
We're thinkin' 'bout buyin' one.

I stop making sandwiches,
open the screen door,
invite them in to take a look.

Nah, but thank you.
He flashes a toothless smile.
Jean, you go on and crawl up in there.

The puffy woman steps inside,
admires the compact kitchen.
This is nice.

She leans over to pet my terrier.
Trooper stretches against her swollen calf,
teeters on his hind legs,
pokes out his tongue to lick her face.

Ain't you sweet.
We're wantin' to take our Lab puppy on trips.
Had to put our 11-year-old dog down.

Jean turns toward the cab,
catches sight of my beagle, asleep
between the driver and passenger seats.

Our dog breathed heavy like that before….

Her words step on a grave.

Later, when I try to lift Toby,
fourteen and lumpy,
he yelps, swings his head 'round to nip,
and his breathing is heavy.

Freestyle

People are dying
        I am swimming.

                People swim
                        I am dying.

                                People sink
                                        I swim.

                                People drown
                        I swim.

        People die
Swim.

I Visit to Help You Pack

February daybreak,
a snowstorm turns everything white,
almost everything   invisible.

A trace of road spurs to West Oaks,
your home, snug
in the Sangre de Cristo Mountains,
where you loved him,
made love with him, where
your soul   his ashes   are rooted.

Your barn house is a shrine—
his worn chair too sacred to sit in,
his drafting board
a makeshift shelf for stilled boots,
his oil paintings:
          a horse, a cactus, you   nude.

This is the place I blossomed.

You crank up his tractor
to plow the road.
I follow in the 4Runner
in case you break down.

After noon, you plant me
in the garden shed where your cat naps
on stacks of National Geographic.
I bundle dust.

In atrium light
where you make your bed,
pots of red geraniums.

Baking Instructions

Take my advice. Think twice
before baking banana bread
one to two hours before
your mother dies.

Yes, the house will smell good
and some literature suggests
chocolate chip cookies or candles
for a pleasurable aroma

or is that a staging device
when you want to sell your home?

Sometimes I am confused.

Clock hands circle … tick, tick, ticking
her hands still … swell, swell, swelling
her breathing labored
for hours now.

No scent or angel forestalls death.
It's coming.
She's going.

Don't do it.

Don't bake banana bread
the morning your mother dies.
It doesn't make anything better.

Aruba

I stop, look at you beside a translucent sea,
reach and remember how to hold your hand.

I forgot your green eyes, the curve of your head,
smooth belly and broad chest.

I tiptoe my fingers along your forearms to your shoulders,
pull you in, tease you away.

I recall how to marry our tongues—moist and able,
imagine my hand straying to the tender side of your thigh.

I take your photograph, barely notice the wind whispering,
one day, it will blow the aroma of you and me away.

Without Children, Pre-Need Arrangements Make Sense

We meet Beth Anne at Asheville Mortuary Services. Tiny pink flowers speckle her silk blouse. Her bangs are bobby-pinned at the peak of her forehead and limp black curls drape her face. The only art in the room is a faded print of a fatigued garden with empty wrought iron chairs, placeholders for souls excused from the table.

Mortality is somber. I imagine an earth sprite tap dancing on the veneer conference table between forms of identification and funereal paperwork. Our parents' names are on those documents, remnants from our birth certificates. Urns inside a curio cabinet witness our signatures and eavesdrop as we name our sister-in-law point person to retrieve our ashes.

Who do we notify when one of us is dead?

Call this number. Beth Anne's bony finger points to a 24/7 answering service. An SUV with frosted windows will ferry a corpse across county lines.

Do you burn the bodies here?

No. The crematorium is a few miles away. Denis makes the appointments. Who is Denis? A death receptionist?

Burial in a national cemetery is free. Death certificates are ten dollars each. Because Mac is a veteran, his copy is gratis. His standard issue headstone is decided—a Latin Cross, Name, Branch of Service, Rank, Born, Died, Beloved Husband, Son, Brother. I will be on the back of the granite marker—Name, Spouse, Born, Died, Be Loved.

All that's left is the dying, sleepy day-to-day activity I take for granted, memory leaking into numbered tomorrows, dissolving and disappearing. Even if Mom and Dad aren't around anymore, we'll be on file together in North Carolina.

Were you a good girl, Vivian?

Wave buh-bye.

Read the Water

Fallen leaves float brown-red on the French Broad
like sailboats on Central Park Conservatory water;
a northern pond, less wild than Carolina rivers.

Flowing northwest against a southbound Greenville Highway,
she glistens gin clear in winter, gurgling and licking rocks,
wears feathered icicles like a boa on the banks of her shoulders.

From static photographs on another Zoom call,
a Pisgah fly fisher woman tries to teach me to read the water.
I will have to sit beside the run to regard the river's body—
riffles and plunge pools, pocket water and back eddies.

Relocating in a pandemic to the foothills, I was never alone.
Butterweed resurrects along a greening shoreline,
a watershed welcome, giddy with rain, spills into spring.

Prodigal Daughter

All I need
is a white shirt,
cotton, long sleeves,
a wool sweater,
easy worn jeans,
warm bread, hot soup,
butter and salt.

Like the son
who squandered his inheritance,
and lived to tell,
I want to return to myself,
who I was before I was
stained. Not proud,
satisfied.

How to Pray in Pittsburgh

Deadhead geraniums early in the day—
new growth is so important.

Plant an orange flame marigold
in silent prayer to the sun,
serving the bee,
pleasing an uncle whose arthritic spine
stops him from kneeling
on the earth.

Warm like a chrysalis
slow and daily.
Wait for wings.
Even if it should rain or hail,
emerge ready.

Come home,
be home,
leave home
again.

Let God watch.
Watch what follows.

Give it a name.

Acknowledgements

Many thanks to the editors and judges of the following poems, some in slightly different form.

Pinesong: "Lea's Wedding Gown"

Witness: Appalachia to Hatteras: "Brown Soldiers" (formerly "Eyebrow Company")

storySouth: "Asymptomatic" — Randall Jarrell Poetry Competition, Honorable Mention, 2022

"Devotion" – The Starkey J. Flythe, Jr., Memorial Prize, South Carolina Poetry Society, Honorable Mention, 2023

"In Anticipation of Winter" — James Applewhite Poetry Prize, *North Carolina Literary Review*, Semifinalist, 2023

North Carolina Literary Review: "I Visit to Help You Pack"

"Without Children, Pre-Need Arrangements Make Sense" — Stephanie Eller Siler Memorial Prize, South Carolina Poetry Society, Honorable Mention, 2023

Broad River Review: "Read the Water"

Heartfelt gratitude to Laure-Anne Bosselaar for her care and clear focus. My thanks to Charlotte Center for Literary Arts co-founders Kathie Collins and Paul Reali for their collaborative vision and artistry, and Lisa Zerkle for administrative excellence. A shout out to Kenneth Chamlee, my mentor in the Gilbert-Chappell Distinguished Poet Series, and Camille Shafer for a residency at Azule. To my "bestest" beta reader, Dr. Natalie Bikulege–Baum. And finally, to my beloved Chapbook Cohort—thank you for helping me to make poetry out of the quicksand of words: Gary Phillips, Linda Vigen Phillips, Betty Ritz Rogers, Brooke Dwojak Lehman, John Clark, Eric Sbarge, Patricia Ann Joslin, Joe Spencer, and last but never least, Lucinda Trew.

And finally, to Dannye Romine Powell, my ferocious friend and teacher. I did not know I would love you.

About the Author

Vivian I. Bikulege is a poet and essayist with an MFA in creative nonfiction from Queens University of Charlotte. A Pushcart Prize nominee, Vivian is published in *The Fourth River, Broad River Review, Presence, storySouth, Pinesong, The Petigru Review, Witness,* and *Catfish Stew.* She was the 2022 Gilbert-Chappell emerging adult poet for western North Carolina, and a 2023 Azule literary resident in Hot Springs, NC. Vivian resides in Brevard, NC with Mac and Trooper, home to white squirrels, terrific trout fishing, and more of God's good people.

www.ingramcontent.com/pod-product-compliance
Lightning Source LLC
Chambersburg PA
CBHW031301120626
46545CB00007B/2922
9781960558084